PREFA

This pocketbook is part of a series _____ _____ and organisations for decency. The aim is to encourage you to look at what is golden and shadow in your work as leaders and as organisations, so people can detox and heal. When we focus on the golden, and address the shadow, then we are more likely to be decent in all we say and do.

Decency is 'honest, polite behaviour that follows accepted moral standards and shows respect for others' (Oxford Learners Dictionary).

We all contribute to what is golden (positive) and shadow (negative) in work and life. Mostly we operate from the golden side, but sometimes we function from the shadow side, and this holds us back as individuals and as organisations. We are all human and fallible.

Let's give ourselves permission to explore the positive and negative so that we create a better balance between the golden and shadow for ourselves and the wider world community. This way, we can contribute to a healthier world both for us now and for the generations to come. And we may yet achieve better decency for us all.

The titles in the Decency Journey Series are:

Healthy Leadership
Healthy Organisations
Coping In A Toxic Environment
Your Own Toxic Work Behaviours
Building an Organisational Mental Health and Well-being Strategy
Volcanoes, Personal Healing and Change
Our Journey for Diversity and Inclusion in Business

Book 4 in the Decency Journey series

YOUR OWN TOXIC WORK BEHAVIOURS

Anna Eliatamby

ISBN: 978-1-80443-013-2

British Library Cataloguing in Publication Data.
A catalogue record for this book is available from the British Library.

This pocketbook also contains some concepts from
Healthy Leadership and Organisations: Beyond the Shadow Side. Anna Eliatamby, Editor. 2022.

CONTENTS

OUR APPROACH

This pocketbook is based on a model that we describe in our book, *Healthy Leadership and Organisations: Beyond the Shadow Side*. Here are the key elements that we use as a basis for this pocketbook.

WHAT IS OVERALL HEALTHINESS?

The words 'healthy' and 'healthiness' usually refer to physical health and, sometimes, mental health and well-being. These facets are important components for overall healthiness, but we suggest that there are others that also must be taken into consideration. These include the degree of synergy between purpose, values, and how life is lived, and work conducted; the impact of material resources and the environment, being willing to be open and listen to the incoming future, and how we live and cope with the shadow side.

All these factors, for overall healthiness, need to be coordinated with compassion and respect by our individual or organisational sense of Self. Collective responsibility for promoting the positive and addressing the negative should be present.

The golden refers to the positive parts of us (kindness, integrity) and of organisations (compassion, working with purpose). The shadow includes dishonesty, bullying, and harassment for individuals and organisations.

Healthiness is an essential ingredient for decency. Without it, we are likely to be unsuccessful.

WHAT IS HEALTHY LEADERSHIP?

Leadership is an individual and collective function that has many intentions. These usually include an aim to serve human beings and/or something else. Some people utilise leadership ethically and positively to serve others. Others will have another focus, such as a profit motive, alongside wanting to be ethical.

Healthy leadership happens when the individual or the group do their utmost to serve others ethically and respectfully while acknowledging that there can be negativity and being willing to address it and heal. They remain flexible and open to sensing the incoming future.

Being and growing as a healthy leader ensures decency in yourself and in how you act at work.

WHAT IS A HEALTHY ORGANISATION?

Why do organisations exist? Usually, it is to enact a greater purpose, which can be forgotten as the organisation becomes bigger and veers from the intended path.

A healthy organisation ensures it remains true to its purpose, and does no harm to humans or the planet. <u>Do no harm</u>. The organisation always endeavours to provide a nourishing culture and structure within which people can grow and flourish in their work to achieve that purpose. A healthy organisation works to recognise and address unhealthy elements, is amenable to change, and is willing to consider possible futures while operating in the present.

Decency is seen as a core essential and its use flows naturally throughout the organization. People do not have to think about the need to be decent, they just are. Thus, the organization contributes to the greater decency we need for the world.

INTRODUCTION

None of us is entirely golden and positive. None of us is entirely shadow and negative. We are all human and fallible—most of us are a blend of both.

We are decent to ourselves and each other and strive for a balance between golden and shadow. But some of us can, for a moment, err onto the shadow side as leaders, e.g., shouting at staff. A few of us will always operate from the shadow side, e.g., bully others because it may be all we know, or we think that that is the best way to manage people.

Often, we don't get or give ourselves the chance to stop and reflect on how we are as leaders, the impact we have, and then consider changing; people rarely give us feedback on how we behave and the effect we have on others. So, we continue in a culture of impunity.

Whoever we are, we must stop and reflect so we can be more decent and supportive of others. This will help our well-being and mental health and that of others. Toxicity has a massive psychological impact on all concerned.

We hope you will take this opportunity to think about what is wonderful about you, about the shadow behaviours you have used, and how you can let them go.

If you give yourself this permission, then you will start on a journey that will benefit you in all aspects of your life. We hope you do.

If you do not, it is understandable. Change, especially as adults, is difficult; sometimes, it is easier to stay as we are rather than change.

If you decide to not try to change, then please make sure that you are operating in a way which does not threaten others' safety and well-being, and that your leadership style does not negatively impact staff.

Here are some exercises and reflections to help you on your journey. We start with some exercises for you to review all your positive aspects.

MY GOLDEN SIDE

You are a senior leader and you have achieved that status through hard work and good use of your talents. But you may not have sat down and thought about what is golden and wonderful about you. This is vital. Here is an exercise to help you.

REFLECTION

Please use one or more of these.

1. First, create a relaxing environment in which you feel safe enough to explore. Where will it be? What is in the space? Who else is there—a supporter or trusted friend or no one? What time would be best for you to explore?

Then write the time and date in your diary.

> *I seriously don't want to do this. But I must and it is time. My manager has told me to stop bullying. I'm going to book an afternoon a week to do this. One exercise a week, pause, reflect. I know it will*

not be comfortable and I could stop. I've told my
partner to keep reminding me how important this
is. She is also sick of how I have been acting.

2. Think about your best, core, or 'sterling' qualities. Here are some questions for you to unearth your 'golden' side.

Which behaviours, emotions, and attitudes represent the best of you?

What would those closest to you say are your sterling and golden qualities? Ask them to write their answers if they want.

3. Now read and reflect on your answers and those of people closest to you. How do you feel?

4. List all the golden behaviours that you possess, even if you do not use them.

Here are some examples: self-esteem, compassion, kindness, decency, optimism, respect, honesty, transparency, humility, integrity, promoting diversity and inclusion, communication, building relationships, collaboration, happiness, courage.

Please use the space below to write a summary.

My golden side

Oh, I had forgotten that I have a good side. It's just that I don't use it that often. I wonder why? Tama, my partner, agrees and says it is a pity I don't use my better side.

VALUES, PURPOSE, AND ETHICS

Most of us can articulate our values, purpose, and ethics. The key difference, especially if we operate from the shadow side, is whether we use them as a guide for how we function in the world.

REFLECTION

What would you say are your core values?

What would you consider to be your purpose—both in your work and your general life?

What do you understand to be your ethics?

How much do you act in line with your core values, purpose, and ethics in your daily life and work?

⟵————————————————————————————————⟶

Not at all   All the time

In what ways do your core values, purpose, and ethics affect how you behave at work and do your job?

> *I say that my values are honesty, integrity, com-passion, and fairness. But why should I reference them all the time in my life? There are many occasions when it is not necessary or possible. I suppose many people are in my position.*

MY SHADOW SIDE

We don't like to think of ourselves as awful people, but sometimes we are—not being patient, letting our insecurities guide how we lead and interact, perhaps even being a bully because we can.

Let's explore.

REFLECTION

Have a look at these shadow behaviours: arrogance, manipulation, cruelty, insincerity, stubbornness, sneakiness, misusing banter, compassion fade/fatigue, hypocrisy, lying/dishonesty, laziness, malicious gossip, prejudice, discrimination, hubris, jealousy, envy, pessimism, competitiveness, vengefulness, psychopathy, sociopathy, Machiavellianism, narcissism, self-sabotage, underperformance, bullying, harassment, fraud, corruption, willful blindness, agnotology, suppression, plagiarism, fear, anger. (The Appendix contains a lot more information about these behaviours.)

Use the table to think about which shadow behaviours you use. How often do you use them? Ensure that this is an accurate picture of yourself. Ask trusted people to verify your views.

Frequency	Shadow behaviour(s)
Daily	
Weekly	
Monthly	

What is the effect of these behaviours on yourself and others? Positive, benign, or malignant?

What would others say about your behaviours? Who do you target? Do you work alone, or have you gathered a group who supports you and uses shadow behaviours?

How do you feel after you have used them?

Note your reflections here.

That was hard. I didn't see or acknowledge how many shadow behaviours I use and how frequently. And how few people I target. When I do, they know it. And, yes, I have my group to help me. We are close and sometimes we discuss who to go for next.

CHARACTERISTICS OF PEOPLE WHO USE SHADOW BEHAVIOURS

People who use such actions are likely to show the following characteristics:

> find it difficult to admit fault, apologise, and change
> tend to deny using toxic behaviours
> function outside social norms and organisational rules
> are emotionally intelligent, charming, and convincing—but focus on self, do not care about their impact on others
> take risks and can be impulsive
> seem immune to the effects of stress
> can bully and harass and use other toxic behaviours.

If, for any reason, you consider that you have any of these qualities, then assess the extent to which your behaviours have a negative impact on yourself and others.

Having some of these characteristics does not automatically mean that you are a psychopath or sociopath or Machiavellian or narcissist, though the qualities listed above are part of those syndromes. But it may help to speak to a mental health professional, such as a clinical psychologist or psychiatrist.

WHERE DO SHADOW BEHAVIOURS COME FROM?

Usually, shadow behaviours originate in your upbringing and background, and relate to people you have met, your relationships, places you have been or lived, and your lived experiences. These influence and shape us, sometimes without our realising it.

REFLECTION

On a large piece of paper, draw a timeline for yourself from birth onwards.

Birth   Now

What types of golden and shadow behaviours did you see being used in the various parts of your life? Whose influence was greatest?

Think of all your environments as you grew up. What influence did they have? For example, did your school encourage you to be considerate, or were negative behaviours part of your experience? What did you learn from toxic leaders and colleagues?

Based on this analysis, where did you learn your repertoire of shadow behaviours?

Oh, goodness, I am so like my mother. She didn't care and just looked out for herself, like me. And then my first three managers were awful, but I saw that they were successful. My style is so like theirs and it works. I don't care about the complaints.

TRIGGERS AND CURRENT USE

Your background can explain how you developed your repertoire of golden and shadow behaviours, and that is worth knowing. It is equally important to understand the underlying reasons for why you maintain your current behaviour.

REFLECTION

Think about your current shadow and golden behaviours—what triggers their use?

Possible triggers could include habit, being competitive, ambition, insecurity, tiredness, not knowing how to manage people democratically, a toxic culture.

For example, you could be in a work environment that encourages such actions. Alternatively, you feel insecure with your team, and you want to feel confident and control them.

Please note your answers here.

Oh, my triggers are feeling insecure and wanting to fit in. If I want to succeed, I have no other option than to really dominate and manage the team. All the other managers do the same, except for Winston who is just weak.

REASONS FOR USING SHADOW BEHAVIOURS

Only a very few of us will use toxic behaviours because we are sure of ourselves and want to utilize them. Indeed, such individuals like the effect of these behaviours and are very comfortable in using them. Most of us have other reasons for using shadow actions, even if occasionally.

It can be difficult to realise that we are acting negatively because often people fear us and will not give us any feedback. We must pause and consider how much we use shadow behaviours and why.

REFLECTION

Think about why you use toxic behaviours. Here are some plausible reasons. Which ones fit you?

Without them, I feel insecure.
I don't know what else to do.
Leading staff means controlling them.
I want to keep people at a distance.
These behaviours work for me, regardless of their impact.
I want to be the winner and the best.

I know better than them, and they need to be put in their place.

Revenge is always the best option.

This is what I have learned, and it works.

I like the effect these actions have on others.

Well, my way must work, because no one has said otherwise.

I like the power that these behaviours give me.

I learned this from my previous leaders and managers.

My family uses these behaviours, so what is the problem?

What have you learned about why you use negative behaviours?

Would your closest and most trusted friend agree with you?

I really don't like people. And I am using what I know. We are on target. So why change? Joja disagrees and tells me it is how I get the job of leading done that is important.

How do you justify your continued use of shadow behaviours? What stories do you tell yourself to maintain your actions?

WHAT HAVE YOU LEARNED?

Pause and think about what you have learned so far about your positives and negatives.

What needs to change?

What needs to stay the same?

How ready and willing are you to change?

If you are ready, then please proceed with the next part of the pocketbook. If you are not, then wait and set a time to come back and think about the issues again and see if it will then be time to proceed.

> *If I want to succeed, then I must change. My director has said so. If I am honest, I am frightened. I'll try.*

❧

> *They are wrong, but I must do these reflections. The most they can expect from me is better behaviour. They will not change me internally.*

DEVELOPING A
BETTER BALANCE

Here are some steps to take so you can achieve a more golden perspective and use shadow behaviours less.

LETTING GO OF THE PAST

We always benefit when we stop, look at the people and events that shaped us, keep what is healthy for us, and let go of what is negative. Try one or more of these reflections.

REFLECTION

Make some time for yourself. Find a place where you feel safe and can relax. Look back over the exercises and create two lists.

Who or what has helped develop your golden side?
Who or what has helped develop your shadow side?

Look at the lists and think of what would still be of benefit and what needs to be left behind.

Cross out the parts that you want to leave. On another piece of paper, write down what you want to keep. Destroy the piece of paper with the shadow side. How do you feel?

For each aspect you want to keep, write what actions you will take to change and how you will maintain the new repertoire of behaviours.

Think of your history from its earliest times. Remember who has influenced you and still does. 'Invite' those who have been positive and helpful to stay and say thank you. 'Ask' those who have been negative influences to leave your life and wish them well.

Imagine placing your negative behaviours in one hand. Rub your hands together to make the negative behaviours disappear permanently. Now imagine washing your hands and cleaning them. Then 'place' your positives in your hands. Look at them and think of a word that will remind you of them. 'Put' the positives in your wallet or purse; store the word in your mind and retrieve it when you revert to negativity. Hopefully, that will help you switch to more positive actions.

EMOTIONS AND EMPATHY

Understanding others and the impact we have on them is important to decrease our use of shadow actions. Enhancing these skills will help us understand the impact our actions have, which can differ greatly from what we intended.

Take some time to learn more about emotional intelligence and its key elements. Perhaps have your emotional intelligence formally assessed. Ensure you use an assessment that is reliable and valid.

How effective are your communication and interaction skills? In her book, *Presence* (2009), Patsy Rodenburg describes three levels at which we can function. On the first level, we are really speaking to ourselves and not paying too much attention to the recipient of our interaction; similarly, the third level is where we loudly focus on our own message. We talk at others.

The second level is the most effective one: you are open to the other person, you pay full attention to them, and you wait until they have finished speaking before working out what you want to say in response.

Those of us who use shadow behaviours are likely to interact at levels one or three. So why not learn about and practise using level two as your primary method? You could read Patsy Rodenburg's book, *Presence*. It is very helpful and includes a lot of useful exercises. You could have some sessions with an actor to rehearse using level two communication.

YOUR TEAM

The people you work with are likely to have gotten used to you and your shadow actions. You will need to convince them you have changed. You can start with a collective apology to the team or provide individual opportunities to discuss your past actions and to express regret.

Having done so, know that it will take time for colleagues to trust that you have really changed. It can take up to a year. Remember to be consistent in your actions, and if you slip back to the old ways, apologise and start again. Sometimes, it can help to ask one or two trusted colleagues to give you regular feedback.

SELF-CARE

Very often, even when we are in balance with our golden and shadow sides, we can forget to look after ourselves and have people in our lives who are like-minded.

Stop for a moment and make sure that you have a good self-care regime that covers all the key areas: physical health, including healthy eating and drinking; sufficient sleep, good well-being and mental health, financial and practical resources, beneficial relationships, and good work habits.

REFLECTION

What can you do to praise yourself more and give yourself gifts? We all deserve these, and they make a difference in our lives.

Consider each of these areas and make sure that you are looking after yourself and maintaining good all-round health.

Self-care	What I do	What more could I do?
Physical health		
Mental health and well-being		
Financial and practical resources		
Beneficial relationships		
Praise and gifts		
Work habits		
Anything else		

VALUES, PURPOSE, AND ETHICS

Return to your statement about your values, purpose, and ethics, and the extent to which they are centre stage in your life. Consider how you could refine them and become more decent.

The Stoics were an ancient group of philosophers with a collective approach toward being values-based and enacting those values in thought and deed.

> *'Waste no more time arguing what*
> *a good man should be. Be one.'*
> Marcus Aurelius, from *Meditations*, written around 180 BC

How can you introduce practices that ensure that you will consider your values and ethics regularly during the day and week? Perhaps start each day by looking ahead and identifying what you will do and say that is values-based. Plan for any tricky moments where you may forget your values and ethics and the need to enact your purpose. What will you do to rectify matters if you err?

Could you develop a self-affirmation that will help to keep you focused on your core? Keep this somewhere safe so that it can remind you of what is important. Perhaps you could have an image on your phone and desktop that prompts you to think of your values. Doing all this will ensure that you do not morally disengage from your actions, which happens when you use toxic behaviours. Focusing on values, ethics, and purpose ensures that you are morally positive.

Setting personal boundaries for what is acceptable—in terms of verbal and non-verbal behaviours—is helpful.

AND FINALLY

Thank you very much for taking this journey. We hope our approach has been of use. Please create your own plan using our guide below.

My positive aspects are…..

How I will address my shadow side…..

My new habits are….

My daily reminders for my new habits are….

If I regress, I will…

I will praise myself by…

My supporters are…

I know I will have made a significant change when I…

I will review my plans and progress on this date…

I have learned to look after myself better and think about others first. I have my plan and Joja is going to help me stick to it. It is possible that I will change internally as well.

❦

I'm still scared but I am using my plan. People have noticed the difference in me. Some are sceptical, but I will carry on. In time, they'll see I have changed.

Thank you. Please contact us if you have any questions.

www.healthyleadership.world
Instagram: healthyleadership.world

REFERENCES

These are available on our website:
www.healthyleadership.world.

APPENDIX

SHADOW BEHAVIOURS, THOUGHTS, AND EMOTIONS

This is an updated extract from the book, *Healthy Leadership and Organisations: Beyond the Shadow Side* (2022).

Banter

What is it? Essentially, it involves teasing others, often in a good-natured way. It serves a purpose at work because it can build social connections and trust. It improves morale and productivity. Acceptable topics of banter include individual characteristics such as age, gender, and personality, but not health, sexual orientation, ethnicity, or faith and religion. Bantering about any of the latter is not acceptable.

Unfortunately, we can misuse banter. If it is malicious and one-sided, there can be a very negative effect on the recipient. They can feel unsafe, lose confidence, and their well-being could be negatively affected.

Often, when someone misuses banter, they claim to have just been joking and that there has been a misunderstanding. However, what needs to be remembered is that it is the impact of their statements that matters the most. It is easy to stop misusing banter; pause, and just think of the potential impact on recipients before saying anything.

For those who are the targets of banter, it is key that they remember their own self-worth and that they can either ask people to stop or report such inappropriateness. What they do will depend on how courageous they feel. It can take years for someone to report inappropriate banter, as happened recently in cricket in England.

Compassion fade/fatigue

This occurs most frequently in human services, such as health and social care and the humanitarian sector, especially for those who work directly with people in dire need, such as migrants, refugees, and very ill people. Professionals working in direct care human services often have great compassion and care, and they give of themselves freely. However, they sometimes must help and work with people who are at the worst points in their lives and may have been through trauma, e.g., disaster survivors. Given that just listening to or reading about another's trauma has an emotional effect on the listener or reader, it should not be surprising that these professionals often develop compassion fade or fatigue. Here, the person almost stops caring and 'tunes out' (as described by Paul Slovic). They become less empathic as a coping mechanism.

People with compassion fade/fatigue are likely to feel exhausted, irritable, forget how to look after themselves, self-medicate, etc. Sometimes, the best option is for the person to leave their work for a while (one to three months), rest and regroup, perhaps see a counsellor, and then come back to work with a more effective range of coping strategies, good social support, and better self-care. Some, however, leave the sector and take up something else.

Hypocrisy

This is the antithesis of integrity; it describes a situation in which someone claims to have and use morals and standards in their work but does not. Many clear examples of this type of behaviour were exposed in 2022. Boris Johnson, ex-Prime Minister of England, and his staff, acted in ways which were contrary to the COVID rules they had given the public.

Jung argues that being hypocritical is an opportunity for the shadow side to emerge. While this is true for some, it is also possible that there are other reasons for hypocrisy. A timid person may be hypocritical to survive in a strenuous life or work situation, e.g., pretending to agree with a project proposal made by a domineering manager only because they want to keep their job. Some may not realise that they are being hypocritical or are that way because their work or community culture demands it.

Some people will avoid being hypocritical because of having to cope with the dissonance that will arise from it. Having been duplicitous, they must reconcile their deeds with their sense of Self, including their values, and for some this can be difficult.

To dissuade yourself from being hypocritical, it is worth reflecting on your own moral code and exploring its boundaries. What would be acceptable transgressions and what would not? Decide on a line that you will not cross, as doing so would mean that you are being hypocritical.

If you are and have been hypocritical, how will you reconcile this with how you see yourself? To whom do you need to apologise?

Lying/dishonesty

Most of us know how to lie and have done so in our lives.

> *I took a break from writing just now and emailed a friend to say that I had sent her vegetables and other healthy food for her birthday present. I did it as a joke, as I had posted chocolates which she loves. But it was a lie that I had written. Does this matter in the grand scheme of life? Probably not, but it could also be a reminder to me of the slippery slope of lying if I then lie in more important areas.*

People lie for many reasons. A desire for material gain can motivate lies, although there probably will be negative consequences such as getting caught. If a person lies out of self-interest, then their behaviour can become a social norm which can be contagious, e.g., describing a controlling and vengeful leader as fantastic even if they are not. We may encourage lying in some organisations, and it can even lead to financial rewards.

There are, however, consequences of lying, even if it makes you feel better. It can deplete you both emotionally and cognitively. You may stop thinking of yourself as a good person, and you may be less trusted.

Sometimes, we lie for compassionate reasons (this is called 'pro-social lying'). If we do, it is possible that people will understand why and see us as still trustworthy and moral, e.g., when we say a colleague looks fantastic even if they are dressed poorly, because they are nervous and just about to go into a very important meeting.

Micro expressions often accompany lying and these can give the person away, e.g., not looking at the speaker, or talking too much. Men are said to lie more than women and younger people more than older ones. People behave more dishonestly when rejected. Very few will lie and cheat to pathological levels; most will lie and cheat a little (Van der Zee et al, 2016).

When does it occur?

Dishonesty is reported to fluctuate during the day—we are more likely to lie as we become more depleted in energy at the end of the day, thus lowering our moral awareness and self-control.

Lying is more likely to happen if we are in situations that facilitate it, such as seeing someone else lie.

There can be a tension between wanting to be a good person versus wanting the benefits of dishonesty, and this will lead to ethical dissonance. If you are effective at justifying dishonest behaviour and still feel good or even better about yourself, then you may be more likely to behave dishonestly in the future.

How to stop

Lying can be discouraged by taking time to see yourself as a moral person and by having a desire to think of yourself positively. What can you learn from your past actions? When were you honest? What can you do to be more honest? What needs to be forgiven?

If you are trying to help someone who is lying, it is important to help them feel comfortable before talking to them about their behaviour. How can you help them relax? Think about how lying became normal for that person. What happened in their history, work, or otherwise? Who/what maintains their behaviour? What has it done to their self-esteem and respect? Having helped the person understand themselves a little more, you should then discuss what other behaviours they could adopt to reinforce their self-esteem and respect in a more positive way.

Prejudice and discrimination

Prejudice refers to the holding of an unjustified and often inaccurate attitude about an individual or group based on a defining characteristic, such as race, culture, or gender fluidity. Discrimination encompasses behaviours (verbal and non-verbal) that are often used against a group about whom a person is prejudiced.

Discrimination is often present, and it is an interesting shadow in all our lives. Few use direct discrimination these days.

> *My most recent example was in a supermarket in Switzerland in 2019. I was waiting in line to check out, and the cashier insisted on telling only the non-white customers (ahead of me) that they had to show her all the contents of all their shopping bags before she would serve them. These were bags containing items purchased legitimately from other shops. When I brought up this issue with the store managers, they said that they weren't sure if this was discriminatory behaviour.*

Nowadays, it is usually indirect discrimination, and that makes it harder to identify it. Here are some examples:

Staff in a shop over-explaining the rules for using the automatic check out systems simply because the customer was non-white

a staff member at a post office, rather than explaining to a non-white customer why it was necessary to complete a form in a particular way, said that they must not understand 'our rules'

These are microaggressions, which have been extensively researched by Professor Derald Wing Sue.

Findings from the American Psychological Association's 2015 *Stress in America* survey showed that those who had faced discrimination rated themselves as more stressed than those who had not faced it. Discrimination could also contribute to the development of anxiety, depression, obesity, high blood pressure, and substance misuse. Discrimination occurs most often in the workplace.

The anticipation of discrimination can also lead to stress, which may negatively affect a person's ability to function in the workplace. They may avoid some situations as they foresee that discrimination may occur.

Discriminatory practices affect job satisfaction, motivation, commitment, and loyalty; staff turnover is likely to be higher. Discrimination can affect reputation and recruitment, and it increases liability, as it is illegal in most jurisdictions.

Dealing with discrimination

It is important to focus on and remember the strengths you possess and your successes. Make sure that you have a strong and supportive network of people. When you can, reflect on what people said in a discriminatory situation, and how you responded. What was good, and what would you like to have done differently? Perhaps rehearse with a trusted friend how you would handle a similar situation in the future.

If you are someone who discriminates

If you have recognised this quality in yourself, stop and think about what your rationale and evidence is for justifying your beliefs and behaviours. Sometimes, people develop biases and associated behaviours because of fear of a supposed unknown, or they may have learned it from a family member or at school or work. Alternatively, they could have picked up their views from the media. It is important to assess what is in the media for veracity and accuracy.

When we act negatively towards another person, we rarely think about the impact of our behaviours and actions on the targeted person or group. If we did, we probably would not carry out the behaviour. Thus, it is vital to stop and think about how you would feel if someone behaved towards you, as you have towards them.

Sometimes, discrimination has a protective function, or it could mean that you want to be seen as part of a group. If this is true, then what else could you do to feel comfortable or be part of the group?

Having reflected, would you change? What help will you need? Which alternative words and behaviours could you rehearse and use? David Olusoga suggests that learning more about other members of our world can be helpful. How will you remind yourself to be more positive?

It is worth it for all of us to explore our views and perspectives and consider whether we could discriminate without realising it.

> *As part of a training session, we asked participants to share all the stereotypes that they knew about people of other nationalities. It was amazing how quickly participants could answer this question.*

What views and stereotypes do you have about people who are or could be different? How do those views influence how you think about and interact with different people? What is positive and negative about your approach? What needs to change?

Hubris

Hubris, as a psychological concept, was most recently articulated by Owen and Davidson (2009). They collated a range of behaviours that can be seen in leaders with substantial power, which is a necessary condition. The behaviours include excessive self-confidence accompanied by a disregard for advice or criticism from others. Individuals with hubris focus on their own self-image and glorification, and they can be reckless and impulsive. They are not that connected to reality, believe they can do no wrong, and can be cruel. People with hubris override anyone else's vision or suggestion and consider that they will always be vindicated.

Such people can be charming, persuasive, willing to take risks, and have an overabundance of self-confidence. Conversely, they can be incompetent, not pay enough attention to detail, cannot listen to others, have clouded judgement, make poor decisions, and have an impaired sense of morals.

Hubris is often an acquired condition which can only arise when a person has power. Repetition of the behaviours maintain them. Tourish (2020) states that these actions, and the associated social field that is created, reinforce the persona of hubris. It can, and usually does, diminish with the loss of power. UK prime ministers, US presidents, and CEOs, amongst others in similar positions, are prone to hubris.

It is very unlikely that those with hubris will seek professional help. There are, however, interventions that can ease its impact. At the individual level, this includes ensuring self-control and self-evaluation, paying attention to others' needs, and allowing others to give you accurate feedback. At the organisational level, we need increased accountability, effective performance appraisal systems, and oversight mechanisms (internal and external) as well as term limits.

Jealousy and envy

Jealousy and envy have some similarities and occur when someone covets what 'belongs' to another, e.g., a partner or an object or a position. Both probably stem from personal insecurities and can lead to the same outcomes as other emotions, such as resentment and anger.

Some argue that these are necessary emotions because they can motivate someone to preserve a relationship. While this has some validity, jealousy can be very wearing on its object.

Symptoms of jealousy can include preoccupation with an issue to the exclusion of all others, and physical signs such as a raised heart rate and sweating. Jealousy and envy can occur both at home and at work. It rarely has a positive impact on the person who is the focus of them.

Research suggests the causes of envy and jealousy include insecurity (poor self-esteem), feeling threatened, fear of abandonment, and trust issues. They can lead to controlling behaviour, damaged relationships, and increased insecurity.

If someone is jealous or envious, they may develop a rationale and justification for their feelings and behaviours. These can vary in severity and intensity, as well as in the extent to which they are real, valid, and rational.

Coping starts with stopping and assessing why you are jealous or envious. What is the validity of those feelings? What is the evidence of their existence? Why did the feeling arise? How can you redirect your feelings and energies into something more positive? For example, instead of resenting a recently promoted colleague, why not look at your CV and plan what you can do to enhance your chances of promotion?

If someone is jealous or envious of you, how valid is their feeling? How did you contribute to it, if at all? How can you engage with the person and develop a different relationship?

Pessimism

> *'The attitude that things will go wrong, and that people's wishes or aims are unlikely to be fulfilled.'*

> *(American Psychological Association)*

Pessimists are likely to expect the negative and become suspicious if the opposite occurs. Signs of a pessimistic attitude include feeling surprised when things work out, thinking that the risks outweigh any benefits, focusing on flaws, engaging in negative self-talk, and assuming all good things will end.

A range of factors can lead to such attitudes including family history and other social and environmental issues. Some people also state that there is a genetic component. Pessimism and its counterpart, optimism, both influence people's cognitions, including their thinking style. They may feel helpless and could be prone to greater stress and have fewer coping skills.

Pessimists could prepare for the worst, but this may adversely affect them. They could have lower self-esteem and be more prone to anxiety and depression. Pessimistic employees can have more negative attitudes which can affect productivity, leading to lower motivation and a limited work ethic. As a result, a blame culture could develop.

Some use the cognitive strategy of defensive pessimism to expect and plan for the 'what ifs.' People who use this strategy can have lower self-esteem and higher levels of anxiety. They set low expectations. Conversely, a strategic optimist will expect that there will be a good outcome, not have detailed plans, and won't be very anxious.

Ways of addressing a pessimistic attitude include learning to hope for the best and plan for the worst, labelling negative thoughts, being realistic, and testing any fears by looking for evidence.

Competitiveness

Being competitive can be helpful, and it has a function; it can lead to greater effort and better performance via physiological and psychological activation. However, its impact depends on the other feelings that arise. If people are fearful and anxious, then they could be less creative and more unethical. If they feel positive and excited, then they can be inventive and more principled.

Positive competition encourages the use of skills and talents without threat. It also unlocks potential and focuses on the capabilities and achievements of all.

How competition makes employees feel is the key: some competitions elicit fear and anxiety because they are based on a threat. If people are anxious, they are less likely to choose innovative behaviours and more likely to be unethical. Other competitions can focus on winning a coveted bonus. This can lead to anticipation and excitement; people are more likely to be ingenious and less likely to be unethical.

When collaboration turns into negative competition, sabotage is much more likely. In extreme competitiveness, the focus shifts from achieving the goal to blocking others. It may lead to decreased effectiveness and an increase in the time it takes for project completion.

Very competitive people only think of the short term because they value winning over efficiency. External factors often motivate hyper-competitive people. If someone has high inner self-esteem, though, then they are less likely to be competitive.

If someone is competitive, it is important to think of ways to collaborate with them, but it may be useful to be wary of trusting the person while continuing to be professional.

If you are competitive, it is worth asking what purpose it serves and whether it encourages trust and cooperation. What could you do to have more collegial relationships?

Revenge

Some will say that revenge is a response to being treated unjustly. You could also be jealous or feel the need for retaliation—you want to make the other person suffer, be exposed for their mistreatment of you, or be forced to stop their behaviour.

Forty-four percent of employees who completed a survey (450 participants), admitted to exacting revenge on a co-worker, e.g., spreading rumours, hiding possessions, getting them fired, sabotaging them, tampering with equipment, eating their food, using information gained from social media, and deleting their work (Insurance Quotes, 2018). This occurred at all levels of seniority.

Reasons for taking revenge included 'making me look bad,' 'was rude or disrespectful,' 'insulting,' 'abused their power,' 'spread rumours,' and 'took credit for my work.' Eighty-three percent of the respondents said that there were no real repercussions. A few said that they had received a written warning or were suspended or fired.

As noted above, vindictive actions can involve the use of social media. Work-related retaliation includes giving a poor performance appraisal, bullying, harassment, spreading rumours, blaming, and threats. Smaller actions, such as purposely not doing what was agreed on, are also possible.

An inflated social confidence and sense of entitlement could produce a desire to take revenge. Neurotics who are likely to ruminate on issues and have experienced anger and hostility can seek revenge years later. You could strive for revenge if you feel you have been rejected socially. However, if you are forgiving, then you are less likely to seek revenge.

People often feel justified in their actions, and such justification can give momentary pleasure, assuage anger, and prove power. Taking revenge does not always lead to the person feeling better and could instead lead to greater anxiety and the risk of retaliation. It is rarely cathartic; the person often continues to focus on the transgressor and the act.

People include revenge/being vengeful in their repertoire of behaviours if they have seen or experienced it in their life. They will find a way of justifying such behaviour, and this belief may not be evidence-based.

If you come across someone who is prone to such actions, it is important to be careful about engaging with them while remaining professional. It is important to learn to recognise the signs of these individuals, such as their taking an intense dislike to someone else with little justification and saying things like, 'I'll get them, just you wait.'

Taking revenge, while perhaps satisfying in the short term, rarely solves much. Perhaps think about what made you take revenge: what was the evidence for feeling that you had to, and how could you address the issue in a more positive way?

Psychopathic and sociopathic behaviours at work

Psychopathy and sociopathy are two subgroups of antisocial personality disorders in the Diagnostic and Statistical Manual (DSM5) which is used to assess people for mental illnesses/distress. There are some differences between the two, largely in terms of the degree to which people use the behaviours described below.

The expected behaviours include not respecting social norms or laws. Such people are prone to lying and deceiving, using false identities, being aggressive, and possibly not considering their own safety. They are very unlikely to feel or show guilt or remorse sincerely. We see such individuals as cold, manipulative, and attempting to control others. They may misuse substances. They may have multiple personas. People with these diagnoses may have limited social skills and find it difficult to manage their anger.

In the work setting, they can charm more senior people but abuse subordinates. They can bully simply because they know how to and enjoy using the associated behaviours. It is estimated that one percent of the general population, and three to four percent of the business world, could be diagnosed as psychopathic.

Successful business psychopaths are more conscientious. This quality is less present in psychopaths who are criminals. Psychopaths can be very charming, have an inflated sense of self, and are good at manipulating others.

Research based on those who are within forensic services shows that people who could be diagnosed as psychopaths often had traumatic upbringings. It is unclear if this also applies to those in the business sector, as they are often subclinical and undiagnosed.

There is also often a big difference between those in the business sector, and those who need help from mental health and forensic services, who show these qualities—the severity of their actions. Behaviours used in the business sector are often low-intensity, high-impact, and high-frequency in nature, e.g., harassment, mobbing, and fraud. Those shown by people with similar tendencies and who use mental health and forensic services are usually high-intensity, high-impact, and low-frequency, such as murder and paedophilia.

It is extremely difficult to help someone change who has these behaviours. The success rate is very low. If someone acknowledges that they have these qualities, then they need to be helped by very experienced mental health professionals.

If you are working with someone who has these qualities, it is important not to take their behaviour personally. It is vital to maintain a professional relationship, but also to be assertive with the person in a polite and non-threatening way so that they cannot intimidate you.

Machiavellianism

Machiavelli was an Italian political philosopher in the late 15th century. Some of his views were extremely controversial, including the idea that deception, dishonesty, and ruthlessness, and even killing innocent people, were necessary tools to achieve and maintain power. It is these views, extolled in his most famous treatise, *The Prince*, that have led to the modern-day description of devious and ruthless business practices as 'Machiavellian.'

Machiavellianism is a personality trait. The salient features are:

indifference in terms of morality
being manipulative and callous
an emphasis on gaining and keeping power by whatever means necessary
planning to achieve personal goals
people high in this characteristic lack morals, appear cold, and are low in emotional empathy and recognition, but not necessarily in emotional intelligence
achievement at the expense of others; may not realise the exact effect of their actions
may not have much insight into their own emotions and may not feel guilt

The Machiavellian at work

Machiavellians function well when there is ambiguity and/or competition. They can initially appear charming. They do not have to be the centre of attention and may prefer being in the background so they can be manipulative. Such individuals are likely to use very negative management approaches.

They are more likely to lie and fabricate in job interviews. At work, they are prone to not share information; they can be arrogant, dominant, and are feared. Research has found that there is a strong correlation between the presence of Machiavellianism and bullying. Individuals with these qualities are also said to function well in political settings.

They will have built these qualities over the years. It is possible that the person has learned them by seeing others, in their childhood or work environment, use these behaviours. They may then feel that these actions are their best option, partly because that is all they know. It is unclear if there is a genetic component. It is possible that someone with Machiavellian qualities could change with support, but they would first need to own the behaviours and acknowledge their impact on others.

It is worth being wary of working with or for someone with these characteristics. You can manage by setting boundaries and being appropriately assertive. Ensure that you look after yourself and build alliances with others in the same situation to support each other, but do not try to counter the negative actions that are presented.

Show and use positive healthy behaviours regardless of those being used by the person with Machiavellian qualities. Be careful about sharing personal or confidential information, as they may use this against you.

Narcissism

Narcissus is a character from Greek mythology who is said to have fallen in love with his own reflection. From this, we have derived the terms 'narcissism' and 'narcissistic.'

Narcissism is a human characteristic in which a person is extremely self-centred in their own needs, concerns, and appearance at the expense of all else. Some behaviours shown include:

    a sense of entitlement
    arrogance
    selfishness
    a lack of concern for others

This is the person who will, if you seek solace from them, turn the discussion to themselves. Sometimes narcissism is a protection for low self-esteem, i.e., an overcompensation. Narcissism, in excess, can be damaging for the narcissist.

The characteristic has similar symptoms to narcissistic personality disorder (classified as a mental illness) but the difference is in its severity and impact on life. People diagnosed as having narcissistic personality disorder can find it extremely difficult to function in life (both personal and work).

As usual, there is speculation about the causes of narcissism. Some say there are genetic reasons, others argue for the role of environmental factors or a combination of both. Some suggest that parenting style can have an effect—from either excessive adoration or criticism.

Some qualities of narcissism can be helpful when becoming a leader, but they can also lead to failure, e.g., not taking others' needs or views into account. Narcissistic employees, if they feel their self-esteem is threatened, may engage in negative behaviours and thoughts, e.g., thinking that others are out to get them. Narcissistic managers and staff will seek external material validation at work, such as having large offices or a huge company car. They often look for constant affirmation, which can be draining.

Professional help can support people with narcissism, but for that to work, they need to acknowledge that they need it. If you are working with someone with these qualities, then it would help to set boundaries and provide appropriate support.

Self-sabotage

Self-sabotage is 'the act of destroying or undermining something, often covertly and directed at yourself' (Mindtools). The behaviours used include procrastination, comfort eating, deliberate self-harm, chronic lateness, and not delivering on time. Negative self-talk can accompany these.

The person carrying out these behaviours may or may not be aware that they are using them. They may have low self-esteem and could be uncomfortable with any actions or events that could elevate them. They could carry out the self-sabotage to continue having a negative perspective of themselves.

People with a background of abuse can self-sabotage, even if they have had professional help. They may be fearful of success or of letting people become too close to them. They may prefer to maintain their status. Sometimes, people who are extremely stressed and have become rigid in their thinking may carry out some actions to sabotage themselves, e.g., saying something rude, apologising, and then being rude again to the person who accepted their apology.

If you are someone who does self-sabotage, it is important to identify the ways in which you do this and try to learn more about what triggers you.

How do you feel immediately after you have sabotaged yourself?

How could you change your response to the triggers?

What can you do to focus on your more positive attributes?

What could be your plan to change and stop self-sabotaging?

Working with someone who self-sabotages can be tiring, irritating, and make you feel sad. Above all, it is important to be supportive of the person, and praise them realistically and not effusively. We should not try to help them analyse their actions, as this could lead to a conflict of interest; there may be some deep underlying issues.

Underperformance

Underperformance is often misconstrued as laziness. It can happen for a variety of reasons—perhaps the underperforming person is under pressure at home, has physical or mental health problems, or is experiencing harassment and bullying at work. Whatever the reason, underperforming usually places the person under severe stress, especially if they are working in a competitive or high-risk environment.

They may be employed to do a job that is beyond their capabilities, e.g., being expected to produce written work in a language in which they are not proficient. A few may deliberately underperform as retaliation because they consider that they have been slighted or not respected.

The first step is to be very sure that the person is underperforming and then have a discussion with them. It is worth taking time in the conversation to reassure the person that the intention is to help, not to punish. Ask them what issues may contribute to their underperformance and how the organisation can help. Once this has happened, there is a duty to help the person get the support they need, consistently.

If the person has deteriorating physical health or mental health, or underlying neuropsychological problems (difficulties reading, writing, etc.), they will need a proper assessment, treatment and social support, and a good return-to-work plan. The person needs to be helped by health professionals first. Managers should only be involved as needed.

Occasionally, a person who is underperforming may find it difficult to trust you, especially if they are being bullied. It would be worth asking them to talk to someone from the internal justice system or the staff representative, if there is one, if they do not want to speak to you.

They may have misunderstood the expectations of their role or find it difficult to meet them. As they are employees, it is important to help them consider the expectations and then work out what extra support or education is needed.

If you are underperforming, it is usually good to stop and think about why, and what help you may need. We all have times when we have underperformed, and it is worth considering what you can do rather than just trying to carry on and making yourself worse.

Bullying and harassment

The UK government defines bullying and harassment as 'behaviour that makes someone feel intimidated or offended' that can 'happen face to face, by letter or email or phone.' Much bullying and harassment is linked to a person's difference from the majority, or their diversity from the 'norm,' such as skin colour, age, disability, sexual or gender orientation, or religious belief.

There are usually laws in place to address the use of these behaviours. They include:

> deliberate aggression, from shouting to constantly criticising someone
> withholding resources
> spreading rumours
> abuse of authority
> denying promotion

An individual or a group (mob) can be relentless in their harassment of an individual.

Most of us could bully if we wanted to, but we choose not to. It is worth remembering this as you read on.

Impact of being bullied

These behaviours may start gradually but can, if not addressed, become continuous and relentless. These behaviours are initiated and thrive in a workplace culture that facilitates them.

The impact of these behaviours can be significant even if they are low in intensity, such as occasional negative comments about work performance made by a manager in quarterly supervision. Obviously, if such behaviours are more frequent and intense, then their impact can be massive, especially if there is cyberbullying, which continues beyond working hours.

The recipient of these behaviours is likely to experience a wide range of emotions, such as helplessness, increased vulnerability, anger/frustration, shock, and lowered confidence. They may also have physical and psychological symptoms such as inability to sleep, headaches, panic, anxiety, stress, family tension, poor concentration, and low morale and productivity.

The workplace is also often affected by increased absenteeism, staff turnover, and costs for providing psychosocial support when these actions are addressed. There are also likely to be decreased productivity and motivation, lower morale, a reduced corporate image, and less customer confidence.

Bullies and harassers seem to identify individuals who lack confidence, are unassertive, and vulnerable. Occasionally, however, they will select someone who is confident but poses a perceived threat.

Qualities of the harasser/bully

Why does someone use these behaviours? Some are insecure in themselves and may not know how else to manage or lead. It is a way of demonstrating power and is an effective tactic to get what they want. They might neither know how nor want to manage in a more democratic, kind, and compassionate manner. Bullies are also likely to disengage morally from their actions (Moore, 2015). They rarely think of the impact of their behaviours on another, and if the recipient becomes upset, they are unlikely to acknowledge their role in eliciting that emotion.

Such individuals could have had a traumatic upbringing or work life, after which they have normalised these behaviours as acceptable. They could be envious or resentful. For example, 'I really don't like Corinne, she is so full of herself.' They may use bullying as protection against some imagined fear.

How to help a bully

Ideally, there should be a substantive range of policies and procedures, and an operational internal justice system in place, to deal with bullying. The policies should be descriptive, and state what we need to address such behaviours as well as what we should do to prevent their occurrence. And, crucially, these policies should be used, not just listed in the policy manuals. Internal justice systems should be trustworthy, otherwise staff will not approach them. Similarly, there should be a person who represents staff to whom staff members can go to for advice. All these interventions need to have full and proper support from leaders and managers.

It is important that bullying is tackled properly, that we give the survivor the help they need, and that they feel safe. Otherwise, the chances of healing and recovery for the survivor are small.

Helping someone who bullies can be very difficult, as it is very unlikely that anyone will have approached them on this issue. Therefore, they have received tacit reinforcement for their behaviours and feel that they can continue. Hence, it is very unlikely that they will believe you when you approach them to discuss their shadow behaviours. Unconsciously, they may be a little wary or scared and so become belligerent. Their behaviours could be their defence and protection.

We can ask bullies to speak to their manager or a coach to address their behaviours. The first step is to be very clear that this is an issue that needs to be dealt with. Consider what will help the person feel comfortable enough to have the discussion. It is worth starting by asking the person what is positive about them and the skills they have.

You can then begin the discussion about their negative behaviours. It is best to have a range of examples of their actions and not just opinions. With each example, it is worth exploring what happened, what impact they felt the behaviour had on the recipient, and what they could do differently. Focusing on specifics is more helpful than just saying, 'Let's talk about your bullying attitude.'

If there is sufficient trust and it is necessary, then there could be an exploration of the reasons for their actions. However, it is important to remember that the intervention described above is essentially coaching and supervision, not counselling.

They may not believe you at first and, even if they agree to change and create a plan (stipulating specific behaviours to use) with you, they may revert to type as a test. It is important to keep having the discussions and reinforce the need for change. They may need extra support to do this. It may be helpful for them to have some sessions with an actor/coach who can help them develop a wider range of behaviours for interacting with others.

How to cope with being bullied

The first and most important thing to realise is that the behaviours being used by a bully say more about them than you. They speak to the character of the perpetrator and not the survivor. However, because bullying can make you feel insecure, it is important to remember your strengths and noble qualities. Perhaps have a picture on your phone that reminds you of who you are as opposed to what is being implied.

If you feel powerful enough, consider approaching someone to talk about these behaviours. They may suggest that you speak to the person and ask them to stop. This will take courage; sometimes it is too much to speak to the perpetrator. If you can speak to them, it will help to rehearse what you want to say with a trusted person. Remember to breathe properly and slowly and to relax. This will help you centre yourself in the discussion. Hopefully, this will be successful. If it is not, then think about what else you could do, such as approaching another, more senior, manager.

If it is not possible to approach anyone, then remember that while you cannot change another's behaviour, you can influence them by how you respond. Practice being quietly assertive; think about different scenarios and rehearse how you will tackle each one differently. It may take some time for you to establish a more assertive presence consistently.

Remember that there can be as much strength in being silent as in speaking up. Sometimes those who are targeted have no other option than to simply get on with their job without addressing the toxicity.

Fraud and corruption

Fraud

We define fraud as 'wrongful or criminal deception intended to result in financial or personal gain' (Oxford English Dictionary). In organisations, the behaviours include bribery, stealing, falsifying documents, extortion, misuse of power and position, and unauthorised use of confidential information. At the individual level, there are many types of fraud, such as scamming, phishing, and identity theft. Martina Dove's book, *The Psychology of Fraud, Persuasion Scam Techniques*, contains an in-depth analysis of fraud at the individual level.

Why do people commit fraud?

Dissatisfied people are more likely to commit fraud, especially if they feel that they have been treated unfairly, e.g., being underpaid. Some may be under financial pressure or feel obliged to a superior who has helped them. Perhaps it is very much part of the organisational culture. A few commit fraud out of sheer greed.

We can describe some as narcissistic who could believe that what they are doing is for the greater good.

The Fraud Diamond provides a good rationale of what can trigger someone to commit fraud. The four necessary elements are: pressure (financial or otherwise); opportunity; rationalisation (sufficient justification); and capability (Wolfe and Hermanson, 2004). If these are all in place and active, then it is highly likely that the person will commit fraud.

Who could be a victim of fraud?

Fraud can be committed in an organisation that has limited rules and regulations or applies them in a *laissez-faire* manner. If there are leaders who either tacitly or overtly condone such behaviour, this then permits fraudulent activity.

At the individual level, fraudsters can target people who are impulsive, have low self-control, are compliant, are easily socially influenced, have limited vigilance, and are susceptible to flattery and intimidation. Dove (see above) has devised a very useful model of fraud susceptibility that is worth considering. The model emphasises the need for the right circumstances and a fraud offer that then interacts with a range of individual characteristics, such as compliance and impulsivity; subsequently, the model has strategies for dealing with the offer, including vulnerability.

Survivors of fraud often blame themselves and are angry, probably stressed, and anxious. What seems to matter most to them is being deceived.

Corruption

This is defined as 'the use of bribery to influence the actions of a public official.' Corruption also refers to 'obtaining private gains from public office through bribes, extortion, and embezzlement of public funds' (Oxford English Dictionary).

Individuals holding power are more likely to act corruptly. Having power can lead to overconfidence, including in decision-making; greater risk acceptance, and a focus on rewards. Overconfidence in their own morality may make individuals less likely to admit or realise that they are acting corruptly.

Those who are powerless may not feel that they can stop corruption if they know about it. If they think they will receive rewards, then they are more likely to be tolerant of corruption.

Corruption is more likely when a person stands to gain personally and has lower self-control. They are also likely to think that corruption will only cause indirect harm and, in organisations, that it is unlikely to be punished. Such individuals are likely to disengage morally and restructure cognitively to justify their behaviours, which will compromise their judgement.

They may also displace responsibility and say that it is the organisation that offers bribes and so it is the organisation that must report the corruption. However, if someone feels guilty, they will be less likely to act corruptly (Anti-Corruption Resource Centre, 2018).

If someone is going to be unethical, it will be more likely if the organisational culture supports such actions. However, if the person has a greater locus of self-control and sophisticated cognitive moral development, then they are more likely to make ethical decisions and less likely to comply with unethical management requests.

Reasons

Corruption can mask insecurities. It could start with a need for recognition, feelings of resentment, or desire for personal gain, financial or otherwise. Being part of a corrupt group can lead to personal recognition. The person could then become loyal to their own values and that of the group. 'You are with us or against us.' They cannot recognise that they are morally bankrupt.

Corruption can have a detrimental effect on mental health. Sharma *et al.* (2021) found that experiencing day-to-day petty corruption was associated with psychological distress.

Growing up with such behaviours being seen as acceptable can lead to someone adopting those behaviours. Their continued use will be facilitated by being in an environment that permits their use.

Prevention of fraud and corruption

At the organisational and national level, there need to be clear and well-understood policies, procedures, and regulations to discourage fraud and corruption. The culture should promote openness and honesty in all. Encourage and reward ethical behaviours. Use integrity measures, such as codes of conduct. Checks need to be made during recruitment for prior dishonest acts and untrustworthiness.

It is also important to ensure that the financial and resource use systems are functional, operational, and reviewed regularly, including the production of understandable reports and exception notifications. Introduce a system (perhaps anonymous) for staff to report discrepancies. Ideally, the organisation should also look at its remuneration packages, so staff are paid as they should be; if so, they will be less likely to steal or become corrupt.

People who commit fraud or are corrupt may be very unlikely to admit to having used these actions, even if there is overwhelming evidence. In such cases, the organisation often terminates the person's employment, and sometimes advises them to seek help to address their issues.

Victims of fraud or corruption may need help to understand that it was not their fault and that we can give them an opportunity to recover. This also applies to teammates of any person who has had their employment terminated, as they will have unresolved feelings.

Wilful blindness, agnotology, and suppression

Wilful blindness

Wilful blindness is a legal term adopted in other sectors. It refers to times when we, as individuals or a group, 'could know, and should know, but don't know because it makes us feel better not to know' (Margaret Heffernan, 2011). Her book, *Wilful Blindness*, describes and analyses many instances in which there was an abundance of wilful blindness, which can occur consciously or unconsciously.

A version of it happens, almost automatically, in everyday life, because there is only so much information we can acknowledge and absorb in each moment. Our attention and other cognitive systems have limited capacity. We must manage the wealth of data that comes into us, and we do this through a variety of mechanisms and filters which are functional but sometimes skewed, especially when stressed.

We can adopt a blindness, especially if there is information that will challenge or contradict our current perspectives or beliefs. We prefer data that confirms our stance and ignores others. In decision-making, this happens quite early.

We could ignore or rationalise away factors that contradict our views. This happens perhaps because of fear of what would happen if we paid attention to such information—besides which, we may want to keep our power.

Inevitably, the truth emerges about these situations, sometimes in very public ways such as it did with the American company Enron. Heffernan describes how and why this happens very well in her book.

Agnotology

Agnotology studies the act of deliberate and culturally induced ignorance or doubt about existing knowledge or science, for someone's benefit. Although we assume that ignorance is the state of not being knowledgeable or not yet knowledgeable, agnotology observes ignorance as a state brought about by individual parties to gain power and profit. People who have backgrounds that promote such actions, or are in circumstances that allow them, are likely to use these behaviours. Here, people manipulate existing scientific knowledge and tools and exploit them to manufacture misdirection and misinformation.

This is a classic example of the manufacture of ignorance from a corporate organisation: a secret memo from the tobacco industry, named *The Smoking and Health Proposal,* was revealed to the public in 1979. Authored in the 1960s by the Brown and Williamson tobacco company, the memo revealed multiple tactics that big tobacco companies used to counter 'anti-cigarette forces.' Regarding marketing tobacco, the memo states:

> *Doubt is our product, since it is the best means of competing with the 'body of fact' that exists in the public's mind. It is also the means of establishing a controversy.*

Tobacco firms spent billions to obscure the facts of health effects from smoking, proactively spreading confusion about whether smoking caused cancer. One strategy used was to declare that studies linking carcinogens to smoking, conducted on mice, did not mean that people were at risk. This created confusion, although it was apparent that smokers experienced many adverse health outcomes.

Interested in the observation that an industry such as Big Tobacco deliberately created confusion regarding scientific knowledge and misled the public to sell a product, a science historian, Robert Proctor, along with a linguist, Iain Boal, coined the neoclassical Greek word for not knowing, '*agnosis,*' and termed the study of wilful acts to spread confusion and deceit, usually to sell a product or win favour, as 'agnotology.'

According to Danah Boyd (2019), such acts of creating doubt and ignorance have power and are a tool of oppression by the powerful. We see this today by some creating ignorance and doubt, e.g., oil companies paying scientists to downplay the effects of climate change.

In the age of social media and the Internet, we observe the purposeful manipulation of science to cast doubt and increase ignorance through data void exploitation. Such media manipulators create a world of content online first, and then drive new terminology through the news media, strategically created to achieve epistemological fragmentation or 'unknowledge' or doubtful knowing about subjects in society, e.g., linking anti-vaccine videos to a news clip which was pro-vaccine.

Some people use social media, news, and blogs to only reconfirm their existing belief system without developing new knowledge, so they remain distracted, especially with repetitive, base entertainment propagating scientific illiteracy, making confusion easier to spread. Actively partnered with the influence of media, governments and corporations can encourage cultural ignorance through secrecy, suppression, document destruction, and selective memory.

Agnotology is a reminder that all organisations and workplaces should reexamine ethics, behaviour, and their impact on the world beyond power and profit.

Ask yourself:

> Do I or does my company work towards something that benefits others?

> What impact do I or my company have on other people?

> Are there any negative implications from my behaviour/my company's behaviour?

Suppression

> *Suppression is defined as* 'the action of suppressing something such as an activity or publication' (Oxford English Dictionary).

Some people will know how to, and do, suppress their emotions and even their thoughts. This ability can be extremely helpful, especially in the care and humanitarian sectors, as it allows you to work and support people even in very difficult circumstances. However, this skill has its limitations. If we use it all the time, then it is very energy-consuming and, eventually, all that has been suppressed is likely to reemerge as cumulative or chronic stress or other mental health problems.

Knowing how to suppress usually comes from life and work experience. For example, growing up in a household where it was expected or working in an environment such as the armed forces, where it is often assumed that you know how to suppress. Some will recognise they suppress but may not appreciate the extent to which they use this ability.

Suppression, as we mentioned above, takes up a lot of energy. It is best to suppress when needed, with a brief immediate acknowledgement, and then release the suppressed emotions and thoughts as soon as possible afterwards.

> *'Oh, my goodness, that was a massive attack on the convoy! Horrible, horrible. Now I need to breathe — inhale, exhale — and coordinate the team so that those involved can get the medical and psychological help they need once they enter our compound.'*

> *'Phew, thank goodness, we have established the response, and the team is working hard to stabilise the injured and stay in touch with families. Now I can retreat, rest, and talk about what happened*

*with my partner and my supervisor. I can let go
of what I have been holding in.'*

How to prevent these factors arising

Counter wilful blindness and agnotology by working to ensure
that there is open and honest internal and external communication in all relationships, and always meet ethical standards.
Leaders should share and endorse expectations. Subordinates
need to see that those who are more senior are adhering to these
expectations. The more diverse the workforce, the better.

Similarly, while suppression has its uses, leaders and organisations
should also create a culture in which staff can suppress when
needed, but also have permission to deal later with the emo-
tionality of the situation, perhaps with professional help. This is
especially important for those who work in emergency situations.

Plagiarism

'Plagiarism is presenting someone else's work or ideas as your own,
with or without their consent, by incorporating it into your work
without full acknowledgement' (Oxford English Dictionary).

With the wealth of information that is available through the
Internet, it is all too easy to plagiarise. Some do not, but others
do. Plagiarism can vary from small amounts to large sections of
someone else's original work. Many famous people have been
accused of plagiarism, including political activist and disability
rights advocate Helen Keller.

On a smaller scale, there is day-to-day plagiarism. Someone in your organisation replicates an old paper under their name; you suggest something in a meeting, and then your manager mentions it to his superiors as his idea.

Legislation on plagiarism exists through copyright laws and other similar statutes. Some are effective and others less so. For example, it is very difficult to copyright a recipe which, arguably, has led to rampant plagiarism by some famous chefs. In fact, you can play a game with this. If you are watching a famous chef on TV and they show and claim an unusual recipe that is not part of their normal repertoire, Google it—you might be surprised to find a very similar one, devised earlier by another, less well-known, chef.

Why do people plagiarise?

There are, of course, a variety of reasons. A person may be lazy yet competitive, so they take the easiest route. They may panic or feel overwhelmed, or do not even think it is an issue or that they will be found out. Some may feel that they lack the knowledge to create their own product, e.g., not being eloquent enough to write in a second language. Plagiarism can ruin a reputation and there may be legal consequences.

Dealing with plagiarism

If a person feels the urge to copy unlawfully, then it is important for them to stop and remember their core values and how they can get the work done honourably. Everyone has ideas and thoughts to contribute. It is worth remembering the guilt that often accompanies plagiarism.

If you think someone is plagiarising, e.g., their written style is very variable, then there are many ways in which you can check. You might use Google and insert one or two key sentences to see what happens. There also are, of course, software programmes that will check for plagiarism.

Fear

The American Psychological Association defines fear as 'a basic, intense emotion aroused by the detection of imminent threat, involving an immediate alarm reaction that mobilises the organism by triggering a set of physiological changes.'

Fear is different from anxiety as it is a short-term response, whereas anxiety is longer-term and future oriented. However, these emotions can be coterminous, at least for the person who is experiencing them. They both have similar symptoms, and whether they indicate anxiety or fear can depend on the label the person and/or others give them. Both can be a component of other mental health issues.

Common symptoms of fear include physical ones such as chest pain, dry mouth, rapid heartbeat, sweating, trembling, shortness of breath, and an upset stomach. There may also be psychological symptoms, such as being upset, feeling out of control, and being overwhelmed.

There can be a degree to which the person experiences fear, and this can vary from trepidation to dread, horror, and terror. We commonly know excess fears as phobias. Specific stimuli can trigger these, such as spiders, or can be unspecific.

The workplace can trigger fears when there is a close link to anxiety and worry. The triggers include job insecurity, e.g., in a recession, or being fearful of a manager or colleague. Fear can then cause effects like those of stress, i.e., lowered cognitive performance and less effective thinking, decision-making, and attention.

There are several therapeutic techniques for understanding and coping with fears. First, it is important to consider the extent to which your fear is having a negative effect and what the triggers are. It is also important to understand what your fear reaction is, from the moment you experience the trigger to the aftermath. You can then consider what alternative responses you could use when you experience the trigger. It can help to rehearse the new responses and learn about proper breathing, which can be helpful in calming down.

Flooding is an alternative approach, in which a person is overexposed to their fear-inducing stimulus. The theory is that flooding will lead to a decrease and attenuation of the fear response. This is a very strong approach and can traumatise the person. We are still waiting for full proof of its effectiveness.

Anger

Anger is a normal human emotion, which varies from mild to severe. It triggers physical and emotional responses. This emotion drives up heart rate and blood pressure and releases increased levels of adrenaline and cortisol. It is an active emotion, driving us to respond to a situation. It is healthy to feel anger—it can provide us with the motivation we need to act against a wrongdoing or injustice, for example. But anger also risks lowering inhibitions and can make us act inappropriately, aggressively, and even violently. It's important that we learn to control and constructively channel our anger, to protect our own emotional resilience, and to ensure it does not become destructive.

Psychological studies have shown that some people get angry more easily and more intensely than others. Such people have what psychologists refer to as a low tolerance for frustration. They feel they should not have to be subjected to frustration, inconvenience, or annoyance—even if everyone else is. They can't take things in their stride, and they get particularly infuriated if they feel a situation is unjust. Their inability to handle their anger or channel it constructively may affect their personal relationships, their ability to act calmly and professionally at work, and their capacity to navigate the everyday challenges of life like traffic congestion, or inefficient bureaucracy, or the multitude of daily setbacks that make life seem unfair.

To manage anger effectively is not to suppress it. It is healthy to express angry feelings in a calm, assertive, nonconfrontational manner. This requires keeping our emotions in control, being respectful of ourselves and others, and articulating clearly what it is we are angry about—without hurting, insulting, or trying to control the response of anyone else.

In contrast, if we do not confront and channel our anger constructively, and suppress it instead, it will continue to fester. This can lead to unhealthy responses, including passive-aggressive behaviour, as well as a tendency to cynicism, hostility, and perpetual grumpiness. It can also lead to side effects, such as problems with blood pressure or depression.

Anger management aims to reduce both the emotional and physical responses caused by anger. It recognises that while it is not possible to get rid of, or completely avoid, what or who makes us angry, we can tailor our responses.

In the text below, we consider some useful techniques to address anger.

Rational and logical thinking

When we are angry, we often exaggerate and overly dramatise the situation or problem we're confronting. We can learn to replace these responses with more logical, problem-solving ones. For example, we can persuade ourselves to recognise that while something is deeply frustrating and upsetting, it is not a disaster, and getting angry won't help resolve the problem.

We can learn to remind ourselves that angry responses alienate or humiliate the people we need to help us get to a solution and will therefore only exacerbate our problem. We can teach ourselves that as much as we want and insist upon being fair and gaining agreement, everyone else may feel the same; we are all equally hurt and disappointed when do not get what we want. We need to learn to ask for and strive for things, rather than demand them as our due.

Problem solving

Sometimes, our anger is driven by the feeling of being over-whelmed or helpless in the face of very real and inescapable prob-lems. Occasionally, we can't hope to find a solution right away. But we can learn to face and tackle the problem effectively, and work towards a solution, taking one step at a time, and bringing others along with us.

Calming and controlling outward behaviour and internal responses

Simple relaxation tools, such as deep breathing and visualisation, can be calming. We can learn and practise these techniques, so that we can use them automatically in a tense situation.

Thinking before speaking

When angry, our words can escalate the situation, and we will later regret what we have said. Managing our anger requires us to take a moment to think through our responses, pause, and then speak. It also necessitates listening to what others are saying and trying to see their point of view. It's natural to feel defensive when we're criticised—but it's much more helpful to listen to the criticism, understand where it's coming from, and respond rationally, rather than leap immediately to aggression and defensiveness.

Using humour

This can remind us to not take ourselves too seriously, get a more balanced perspective, and face our reactions more constructively. Sometimes, all it takes is to imagine yourself as an external observer, watching the crazy person (yourself) losing your cool to no avail, to be reminded that anger is more likely to elicit laughter or scorn than sympathy and help.

Take time out

Sometimes, we need to give ourselves a break, some personal quiet time, to help us then deal with situations or people more calmly.

Physical activity

Physical activity can help to lower high stress levels, which can trigger anger. It can also provide an immediate release for angry feelings—if you feel your anger escalating, a slow walk could help to calm you down.

Know your triggers

If you are more likely to get angry in the evening when you're tired, for example, or if a colleague repeatedly presents you with a problem first thing in the morning before you have even reached our desk—you could communicate these triggers to those around you, and plan so that problems and difficult conversations take place at more constructive moments in the day.

Pick your battles

If you can, avoid the things that you know will infuriate you. For example, if your daily commute leaves you enraged by the time you reach the office, try to find an alternative route that is less congested or noisy, or leave earlier to miss some of the traffic.

Other toxic behaviours, thoughts, and emotions

Used persistently, these behaviours, thoughts, and emotions (described above and below) can have a very negative and serious impact on the well-being and mental health of individuals and groups. Consistent displays of related actions can lead to toxic work environments; some people may even normalise these behaviours and, perversely, see them as acceptable.

Such environments, especially if the toxicity is covertly or overtly condoned by leaders and managers, can have adverse effects on productivity and lead to higher levels of stress and anxiety. Sometimes, employees will seek refuge through the internal justice system which can help; but unfortunately, using them may lead to further problems, such as the targeting of whistle-blowers.

As well as the behaviours, thoughts, and emotions outlined above, toxic behaviours include:

manipulation

cruelty to others, e.g., being invited to and then refused entry to a leaving party

cheating in interviews

having someone else do your written test

Toxic behaviours also include those labelled as 'master suppression techniques,' aimed at quashing or dominating another. Ingjald Nissen initially identified nine, which were then reduced to five:

making someone feel invisible/silencing/claiming another's work

ridiculing someone

withholding information

double punishment

blaming or shaming someone

These actions occur for a variety of reasons, such as resentment, jealousy, competitiveness, and insecurity. Some people use these actions deliberately.

Interventions

If you have used any of these behaviours, then stop and think about their impact on the receiver, and what led you to use them. How would others describe you? Positively or negatively? How can you address your feelings, e.g., being competitive or jealous, more positively?

If others have subjected you to toxic behaviours, it is important to recognise that such actions say much more about the other person than about you. It is important to rethink how you could have approached those situations. How assertive were you? What happened, and how could you be more assertive next time? How can you detach yourself from these situations? Remember, as David Sheff said, 'I didn't cause it. I can't control it. I can't cure it.' You can, however, manage how you respond.

Review your coping strategies, both in life and at work. Perhaps limit how much time you spend with those who use toxic behaviours. Try to establish some boundaries, such as asking them to be polite when speaking to you. They may not believe you at first because, probably, no one else has had the courage to confront them. It is important to be as calm and as centred as possible.

None of us can change another's behaviour, but we can control how we respond to them, and help to create an atmosphere where people do not accept that person's negative behaviours.

How can you work with others to create a positive work environment in which it will be very difficult for toxic behaviours to be used? For example, you could provide feedback for such behaviours, and expect honesty and openness from all.

Printed in Great Britain
by Amazon

15977980R10058